Journey through
Ellis Island

THIS EDITION

Editorial Management by Oriel Square
Produced for DK by WonderLab Group LLC
Jennifer Emmett, Erica Green, Kate Hale, *Founders*

Editor Maya Myers; **Photography Editor** Nicole DiMella; **Managing Editor** Rachel Houghton;
Designers Project Design Company; **Researcher** Michelle Harris;
Copy Editor Lori Merritt; **Indexer** Connie Binder; **Proofreader** Susan K. Hom;
Sensitivity Reader Ebonye Gussine Wilkins; **Series Reading Specialist** Dr. Jennifer Albro

First American Edition, 2024
Published in the United States by DK Publishing, a division of Penguin Random House LLC
1745 Broadway, 20th Floor, New York, NY 10019

Copyright © 2024 Dorling Kindersley Limited
24 25 26 27 10 9 8 7 6 5 4 3 2 1
001–339772-Mar/2024

All rights reserved.
Without limiting the rights under the copyright reserved above, no part of this publication may be reproduced, stored in or introduced into a retrieval system, or transmitted, in any form, or by any means (electronic, mechanical, photocopying, recording, or otherwise), without the prior written permission of the copyright owner.
Published in Great Britain by Dorling Kindersley Limited

A catalog record for this book is available from the Library of Congress.
HC ISBN: 978-0-7440-9434-3
PB ISBN: 978-0-7440-9433-6

DK books are available at special discounts when purchased in bulk for sales promotions, premiums, fund-raising, or educational use. For details, contact:
DK Publishing Special Markets, 1745 Broadway, 20th Floor, New York, NY 10019
SpecialSales@dk.com

Printed and bound in China

The publisher would like to thank the following for their kind permission to reproduce their images: a=above; c=center; b=below; l=left; r=right; t=top; b/g=background

Alamy Stock Photo: Archive Collection 26r, Associated Press / Anonymous 50tl, Contraband Collection 46, Everett Collection Historical 14b, Terese Loeb Kreuzer 59rl, Magite Historic 38, North Wind Picture Archives 7tr, Science History Images 15t, Science History Images / Photo Researchers 55br, Scherl / Sddeutsche Zeitung Photo 8tl, Vintage*Kids 11tr; **Bridgeman Images:** Granger 35tl, Look and Learn / Elgar Collection 16tl; **Courtesy Megan Smolenyak:** colorization by Dimple Negi 6cla; **Dreamstime.com:** Baibaz 58tl, Mark Gusev 52bl, Christopher Howells 30cl, Felix Mizioznikov 4-5, Sean Pavone 60bl, Stockshooter 8bl, Taniavlad 59br, Vladvitek 19tr, Vladimir Voronin 37tr; **Getty Images:** AFP / Kena Betancur / Stringer 60-61, Archive Photos / Fotosearch / Stringer 43cra, Archive Photos / Frederic Lewis / Staff 44-45t, Archive Photos / Graphic House / Staff 33, Archive Photos / Hulton Archive / Stringer 19tl, Archive Photos / Jim Heimann Collection 14tl, Archive Photos / Museum of the City of New York / Jacob A. Riis 48-49, 52tl, Archive Photos / PhotoQuest 53, Archive Photos / Smith Collection / Gado 9b, Bettmann 9tr, 10c, 12br, 18br, 24tl, 26tl, 36tl, 44tl, 47, 54bl, Corbis Historical / Fine Art / VCG Wilson 31, Corbis Historical / Historical 39bl, Corbis Historical / Michael Maslan 56-57b, Hulton Archive / Ann Ronan Pictures / Print Collector 24-25b, Hulton Archive / Apic 42-43, Hulton Archive / brandstaetter images / Imagno 22, Hulton Archive / Historica Graphica Collection / Heritage Images 28-29t, Hulton Archive / Staff 28-29b, Hulton Fine Art Collection / Fine Art Images / Heritage Images 16-17t, Keystone View Company / FPG / Staff / Archive Photos / Hulton Archive 58br, SeM / Universal Images Group 3, Universal History Archive / Universal Images Group 20tl, 40tl, Universal Images Group / Photo 12 35bl, Nick Ut 23br, George H. Davis, Jr. / Library of Congress / Corbis / VCG 57tr; **Getty Images / iStock:** LeonU 60tl, Nerthuz 39tc; **Library of Congress, Washington, D.C.:** LC-DIG-ds-13992 10tl, LC-DIG-ggbain-50437 / Bain News Service, Publisher 13bl, LC-DIG-ppmsc-00157 36–37b, LC-DIG-ppmsca-53147 15crb, LC-DIG-ppmsca-58667 32; **Courtesy of National Park Service, USA:** 10cr, 10br, 11tl, 48tl, 49br; The New York Public Library: Manuscripts and Archives Division, The New York Public Library. "Three women from Guadeloupe" The New York Public Library Digital Collections. 1906–1914. https://digitalcollections.nypl.org/items/510d47de-79d6-a3d9-e040-e00a18064a99 34, Rare Book Division, The New York Public Library. "ABEND–ESSEN [held by] HAMBURG–AMERIKA LINIE [at] "AN BORD DER ""AMERIKA""" (SS;)" The New York Public Library Digital Collections. 1906. https://digitalcollections.nypl.org/items/510d47db-7e77-a3d9-e040-e00a18064a99 40br, The Miriam and Ira D. Wallach Division of Art, Prints and Photographs: Photography Collection, The New York Public Library. "Joys and sorrows at Ellis Island, 1905" The New York Public Library Digital Collections. 1905. https://digitalcollections.nypl.org/items/510d47d9-4e7a-a3d9-e040-e00a18064a99 11cl, 13tl, 50-51b, The Miriam and Ira D. Wallach Division of Art, Prints and Photographs: Picture Collection, The New York Public Library. "Ellis Island, New York City" The New York Public Library Digital Collections. 1906. https://digitalcollections.nypl.org/items/510d47e2-8c4f-a3d9-e040-e00a18064a99 1, 27, 42tl; **Shutterstock.com:** Everett Collection 21l, 40-41t, 55tl, Frontpage 12t, Oleksandr_U 17br, TTstudio 6-7; **The US National Archives and Records Administration:** 7cl, 8-9tc, 23tl, 30b, 56br; **US Patent and Trademark Office:** 54tl

Cover images: Front: **Library of Congress, Washington, D.C.:** LC-DIG-fsa-8e11208/Hine, Lewis Wickes, photographer;
Back: **Dreamstime.com:** Dibrova clb, Vladimir Voronin cra

All other images © Dorling Kindersley
For more information see: www.dkimages.com

www.dk.com

This book was made with Forest Stewardship Council™ certified paper – one small step in DK's commitment to a sustainable future.
Learn more at
www.dk.com/uk/information/sustainability

Level 4

Journey through Ellis Island

Paige Towler

CONTENTS

6	Exploring Ellis Island
14	Leaving Home
24	Destination: USA
32	The Journey to Ellis Island
42	Ellis Island at Last

52 A New Life
62 Glossary
63 Index
64 Quiz

EXPLORING ELLIS ISLAND

On New Year's Day, 1892, a teenage girl from Ireland made history by stepping onto a small island in New York Harbor. Today, a visitor might not think much of this island with some trees and a handful of buildings. But for this girl, it was monumental.

The Ellis Island Immigration Station as it appears today

Her name was Annie Moore, and she was an immigrant, a person who moves to live permanently in a country they were not born in. Annie was the first-ever person to immigrate to the US through this island: Ellis Island.

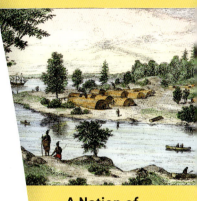

A Nation of Immigrants
The land that would become the United States was home to many Indigenous peoples for thousands of years before Europeans arrived in the 16th century. The land's first immigrants were invaders who colonized Indigenous nations. Before the 16th century, the lands around what is now Ellis Island were home to the Lenape people.

The original Ellis Island Immigration Station building, which was destroyed by fire in 1897

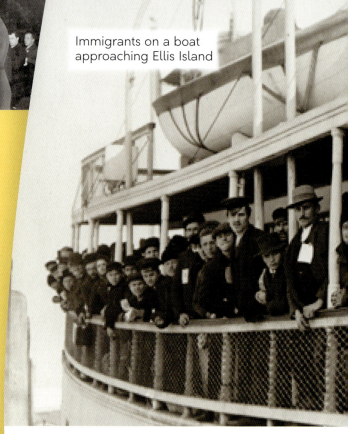

Immigrants on a boat approaching Ellis Island

Lots of Languages
Interpreters of at least 23 languages worked at Ellis Island to help people communicate. Interpreters had to pass an exam that proved they could speak, read, and write in both English and another language.

A Welcome Sight
Just southwest of Ellis Island, Annie Moore would have spotted a famous sight: the Statue of Liberty, on Liberty Island.

To reach Ellis Island, Annie and her two younger brothers had traveled across the Atlantic Ocean. After 12 long days at sea, they had finally arrived. They were likely nervous because they had made the trip without their parents. But they were probably excited, too! Ellis Island would change their lives forever.

8

Americans, Immigrants, or Both?

When Annie arrived in the US, many people who lived in America would have considered her an immigrant, while they thought of themselves as Americans. But their ancestors were probably immigrants, too! Today, all Americans except Native Americans are descended from immigrants.

Around Annie, thousands of people filed into a large wooden building. Languages Annie couldn't understand filled the air. Immigrants had come to enter the US from many other countries, just as they had for hundreds of years.

Immigrants arriving at Ellis Island, early 1900s

9

Many people wanted to immigrate to the US. But their immigration had to be approved by US government workers. Ellis Island was one of several official entry points to the US.

Forced Migration

Not all people who came to the US chose to do so. From the 16th to the 19th centuries, Europeans captured and enslaved more than 12 million African people and forcibly transported them to the Americas. These enslaved people were forced to work in inhumane conditions for no money, and they had no freedoms.

Particular Ports
Ellis Island was the closest port to Europe. Travelers from other parts of the world entered the US at different ports. Between 1910 and 1940, many immigrants came through Angel Island, off the coast of San Francisco, California. They came from countries like China, Japan, Australia, New Zealand, and Mexico.

Most people passing through Ellis Island came from countries in Europe. Some huddled with their family members—grandparents, parents, and children. Others traveled by themselves. Some, like Annie and her brothers, were children traveling alone. But they all had the same question: What would their new lives in America be like?

Ellis Island, as seen from New Jersey

Isle of Hope? Around 2 percent of immigrants to Ellis Island were turned away. But for the 250,000 people who were denied entry, the Isle of Hope became the Isle of Tears.

Who was allowed to enter the US, and who was not? And why did so many people want to come to the US? Why did they want to leave their old homes and start new lives? Were Annie and her brothers allowed to stay?

Immigrants arriving at Ellis Island in the early 1900s

Everyone who immigrated to the US had a different journey. For many people, traveling across the world to start a new life was a hopeful voyage tinged with sorrow. What might it have been like to leave behind your old life and home and to travel thousands of miles to a new land?

Little Island, Big Impact
Between 1892 and 1954, Ellis Island received more than 12 million immigrants. About 40 percent of the current US population can trace their heritage through Ellis Island.

Busiest Day
On April 17, 1907, more than 11,000 immigrants came through Ellis Island.

13

LEAVING HOME

People like Annie left behind their friends, home, school, and more. Such a big adventure can be exciting—but also a bit scary. And this journey would have been tough 100 years ago.

Immigrant Spotlight: Thomas Family
Diab Thomas's family—wife Mary and their children, Salene and Alene—came through Ellis Island in 1907. They came from Lebanon and went on to operate a grocery store in West Virginia.

An ocean liner leaves Queenstown, Ireland, for the US around 1903.

Transcontinental Railroad, completed 1869

From the late 1800s through the early 1900s, scientific discoveries and inventions changed how people lived, moved, and communicated. People could share ideas and thoughts in a way that hadn't been possible before. And they could travel long distances faster than ever.

Hello?
In 1876, Alexander Graham Bell—an immigrant from Scotland—created one of the first successful telephones.

Troubles around the World
By the 19th century, China's population had grown so much that both jobs and food were in short supply. Facing heavy taxes, or money owed to the government, many people left to find work in the US.

During the 19th and 20th centuries, life had become difficult in certain parts of the world. In Ireland, Annie's country of origin, there were not many jobs. Most people worked the land as farmers, surviving on the food they grew, mostly potatoes. In 1845, a mold called blight began destroying potato crops.

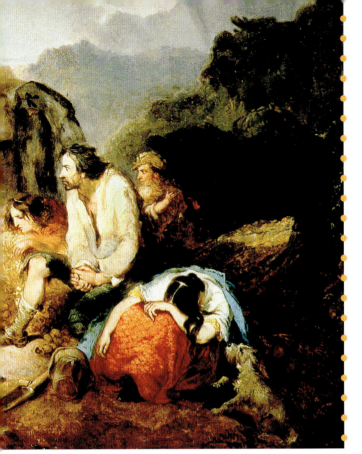

This 1847 painting by Daniel Macdonald shows an Irish family discovering blight in their potatoes.

Early Irish Immigrants
The first Irish immigrants arrived in the Americas long before Ellis Island existed—even before the US existed. Many Irish people arrived in North America's British colonies in the 1700s.

The mold spread, ruining potato crops across Ireland. This became known as the "Great Hunger," or the "Irish Potato Famine." Many people knew that if they stayed, they would starve. So, they gathered their families and set out across the Atlantic Ocean in search of a new home.

Potato with blight

Pizza Party
When immigrants from southern Italy—the birthplace of modern pizza—arrived in the US, they brought their recipes with them.

Many immigrants at Ellis Island came from Italy. During the 19th century, Italian troops battled to drive out foreign leaders who had taken control of parts of the country. In 1861, the Italian troops succeeded, and the wars ended. However, the wars left many people in Italy poor or even without homes.

Immigrants from Italy at Ellis Island, 1905

Messina, Italy, after the earthquake, 1908

Life was also difficult in southern Italy. In the 1800s, the volcano Mount Vesuvius erupted multiple times, destroying farms and homes. In 1908, a powerful earthquake triggered a giant tsunami that caused more damage. People hoped they could build better lives in other places. They made the brave decision to journey to foreign lands.

Immigrant Spotlight: Tilda de Mello Kelly-Grimm
Tilda de Mello Kelly-Grimm immigrated twice! She was born in Brazil in 1917. At age four, she got malaria, a disease spread by mosquitoes, which were common in Brazil. To avoid the illness, her family moved to Portugal. In 1925, they left Portugal for the US, hoping to find opportunities for work.

Jewish immigrants from Russia or Ukraine arriving in the US, circa 1900

> **Immigrant Spotlight: Chadekel Family**
> In 1909, pogroms broke out in Lithuania. Barnett and Chann Chadekel, who were Jewish, traveled with their children in secret to Germany, where they boarded a ship that carried them safely to Ellis Island.

In Eastern Europe, Jewish people faced antisemitism. Antisemitism is a form of prejudice, or hatred and discrimination, against people of the Jewish faith. Antisemitism led people to target Jews. Beginning in the late 1800s, Jewish people suffered violent mob attacks called pogroms. Many Jews feared for their safety and their lives.

Because of antisemitism, countless Jewish people were forced to leave their homes. Beginning in the 1880s, many Jewish families fled to the US, where laws granting religious freedom made it easier to safely start new lives. By 1924, more than two million Jews had immigrated to the US in search of brighter futures.

Bringing the Bagel

For centuries, Jewish people in Poland and Germany have enjoyed a round bread that is first boiled and then baked. Many Polish Jews settled in New York City, where the bread now known as bagels were a hit.

Jewish men and boys in front of a tenement synagogue in New York City on Yom Kippur, around 1910

Escaping Danger
Immigrants who leave their home countries to escape dangerous situations are called refugees. Many Jewish people immigrating to the US were refugees.

Whatever people's reason for immigrating, leaving their homes probably wasn't easy. They had to leave behind most of their belongings. Some had to leave in secret or in a rush, bringing only what they could grab.

Refugees in Poland, around 1918

Immigrants arriving at Angel Island, 1939

Emigration Today

Even though the world is different today, people still emigrate, or move away, from their home countries for many of the same reasons others did more than a century ago. Many current refugees are escaping unsafe conditions, like war, violence, and natural disasters.

Most people who decided to leave their homes were hoping to make their lives better. They struck out for the US, a faraway place with new customs, new rules, and in most cases, a different language. Before they could learn these new ways of life, they had a long, hard journey ahead.

Migrants attempting to enter the US from Mexico, 2023

Gold Rush!
In 1848, gold was discovered in California. People flooded into the state in hopes of striking it rich.

Opportunity for Some
Not all people had access to the same opportunities in the US. Until 1865, the enslavement of Black people was legal. Indigenous people, who had inhabited the land for thousands of years before European settlers arrived, were forcibly relocated and often killed, both by early settlers and the US government.

DESTINATION: USA

Between 1815 and 1915, more than 30 million people immigrated to the US. Nearly half those immigrants came through Ellis Island. Why did so many choose to come to the US? One big reason was the US economy, or the country's system of spending and creating money and goods. The economy was doing very well, so jobs were plentiful.

The 19th century brought big changes to the US. New inventions and technologies created new jobs. The US was still expanding westward. For immigrants who did not have opportunities to change their circumstances at home, the US seemed like a great place to start over.

Immigrant Spotlight: Jue Family
In the 1880s, tales of life in California inspired Tong Ly Jue to try his luck in a new land. From Canton, China, Jue immigrated through Angel Island. He became an herbalist in San Francisco.

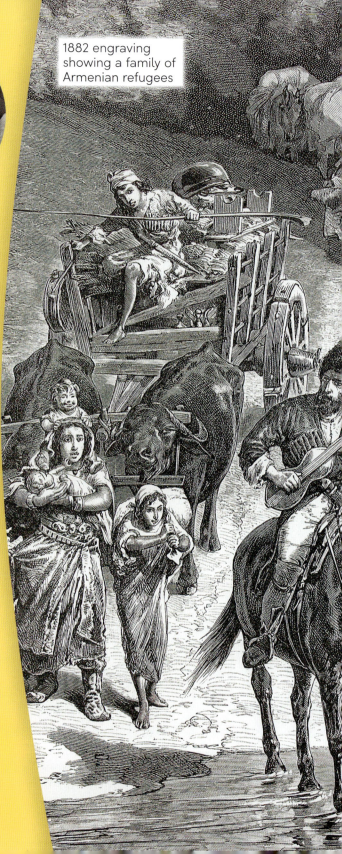

1882 engraving showing a family of Armenian refugees

Facing Persecution

Many Armenians faced persecution under the Ottoman Empire, which ruled parts of Europe and the Middle East from the 15th century to the early 20th century. Beginning in the 1890s, this persecution grew into violence and ultimately genocide, or the widespread killing of Armenians. To escape the danger, many Armenians immigrated to the US.

Wealth was not the only reason people chose to journey to the US. When the US was founded, its rules included a promise of religious freedom. This meant that any US citizen had the freedom and safety to practice any religion, or none at all. For people who could not safely worship in their home countries, the US symbolized safety.

Some people chose to move to a certain part of the US because other immigrants had already moved there. In some cases, as with Annie Moore's family, after one or more family members moved to the US, others followed. Some immigrants wanted the support of an established community of people from their home country.

Family Reunion
Why were Annie Moore and her brothers traveling alone? The rest of their family had already moved to the US.

Finding Community
Some communities encouraged connections through churches and other places of worship. Others offered work opportunities. For example, many Chinese American restaurants trained newly arrived Chinese immigrants to cook and work as servers.

Chinese restaurant, New York, early 20th century

1887 illustration of the grounds and port in front of Castle Garden

Other Destinations
During the 19th and 20th centuries, Canada, Argentina, Brazil, and Australia also experienced large waves of immigration.

For much of the 1800s, each US state was in control of its own immigration. New York received immigrants in a fort called Castle Garden (now known as Castle Clinton) in New York City. As more and more immigrants arrived, it became clear that Castle Garden could not handle such large numbers.

Immigrants with their luggage outside Castle Garden, 1880s

To help smooth out the immigration process, the US government decided to open federal, or government-owned, immigration ports. On the East Coast, the busy and popular New York City seemed like a logical spot to receive ships crossing the Atlantic Ocean from European countries.

What's in a Name?
Ellis Island was once known as Kioshk, or "Gull Island," by the Lenape people. In the 1600s, Dutch colonists seized control of the island, calling it Oyster Island due to its many oysters. The small piece of land passed hands several times in the next century before being purchased by businessman Samuel Ellis in the 1770s.

Year One
In the first year of its opening, some 450,000 immigrants arrived at the Ellis Island Immigration Station.

Fire!
In 1897, just five years after the Ellis Island station opened, a fire ravaged the original wood structures and destroyed the immigration records from those five years. With new brick buildings, the immigration station reopened in 1900.

Ellis Island passed from the Ellis family to the John A. Berry family before the US government purchased it in 1808 for $10,000. The government intended to use the small island as a harbor defense—but at first, ships just dumped their trash there! Over the years, more land was built up on the dumping grounds around the island. This empty island just off New York City seemed like the perfect spot to receive arriving ships. In 1892, the Ellis Island Immigration Station officially opened.

Construction of the Ellis Island Immigration Station, January 11, 1900

Castle Garden, at the Port of New York, 1852

THE JOURNEY TO ELLIS ISLAND

Today, to travel a very long distance, you would probably fly in an airplane. But in 1892, the only way to travel across the Atlantic Ocean was by ship. For centuries, people had relied on the wind and ships with sails to travel across the ocean. But an invention from the early 1700s changed everything.

Immigrant Spotlight: Edward Hong Although most Chinese immigrants traveled through Angel Island, they did not all settle on the West Coast. Eight-year-old Edward Hong immigrated to the US in 1923 with his family, and they moved to Illinois. After growing up there, he served as a soldier in World War II and then became a lawyer and state assemblyman in New York City.

Around 1712, a British inventor devised an engine that used steam to create energy. In the early 1800s, engineers created steam locomotives—some of the world's first trains. Steam engines were also used to power steamships, which traveled much faster than sailing ships. They could also travel against ocean currents. But even on a steamship, the journey to the US was much longer—and harder—than it is today.

Full Steam Ahead
In 1863, two US railroad companies began building the Transcontinental Railroad—the first railroad line that ran across the whole US. The railroad was completed in 1869, thanks in large part to the labor of Chinese, German, and Irish immigrants.

Immigrant Spotlight: Ella Dowleyne
Ella Dowleyne was 15 years old when she set out alone from Barbados for Ellis Island in 1907. She would live with her sister, who had immigrated to New York in 1905 and felt that the US offered more opportunity than their small home country.

Immigrants from Guadalupe, 1911

Tickets to travel on the steamships were not hard to come by. In fact, salespeople from ship companies traveled from country to country selling tickets. But affording a ticket was difficult for many people. Some people saved money for weeks, months, or years. Others—like Annie Moore—got tickets from family members already in the US.

Once they had a ticket, most people had to travel to a port city, where they could board a ship. Some, like Annie, already lived near the ocean. But for others, this meant a long journey, by train, in wagons, on donkeys, or even on foot.

The Port of New Orleans

For people immigrating from countries to the south, the closest port was in New Orleans, Louisiana. Beginning in the 1880s, Caribbean and Latin American workers on the Panama Canal immigrated to the US, many through New Orleans. As a hub of Catholicism, New Orleans attracted Catholic immigrants from other countries. For several centuries before this, New Orleans was a primary port where enslaved Africans were brought forcibly into the US.

Toy Time
Children could sometimes bring their most treasured toys on the journey. In the 19th century, they might have had dolls made from cloth and wood or porcelain, as well as marbles, toy soldiers, wooden trains, and jump ropes.

What would you pack for a long, difficult journey—especially if you had to leave most of your things behind? Lots of people, including Annie, could bring only one bag. People packed things they felt were necessary or valuable.

Arriving at Ellis Island

Most people leaving home packed some of their best clothes. They brought tools that might help them find work and items that held memories, like photographs or jewelry. Many carried religious items, such as bibles or menorahs.

This illustration shows the design for the grand staircase on the sister steamships *Titanic* and *Olympic*.

Crossing the Atlantic Ocean on a steamship could take more than a week. For wealthy people, who bought tickets in first or second class, this journey was probably pretty nice! They stayed in private rooms and had access to healthy meals.

Some wealthy people traveled on luxury ship lines. They brought lots of luggage, ate in elegant dining rooms, and had access to the types of activities and entertainment you might find in a fancy hotel—even ballrooms and swimming pools! However, for most emigrants, the journey was much harder.

Doomed Ship
In 1912, the luxury passenger ship *Titanic* set sail from England. It was headed for New York City. On board were some 2,200 passengers and crew, many of whom were immigrants. Tragically, four days after it set sail, *Titanic* struck an iceberg and sank, killing about two-thirds of the people on board.

Past Voyages
Although a week-long voyage might sound tough, it was a fast trip compared to what had come before. In the days of sailing ships, traveling across the Atlantic Ocean took anywhere from six weeks to several months.

Entertainment at Sea
On long voyages, passengers in steerage played card games or spent time talking. Those who'd brought instruments along might have led others in singing and dancing.

People who couldn't afford a luxury voyage—that is, most people—traveled on more affordable shipping boats or on mail and cargo boats called packet ships. The cheapest passenger section was called steerage.

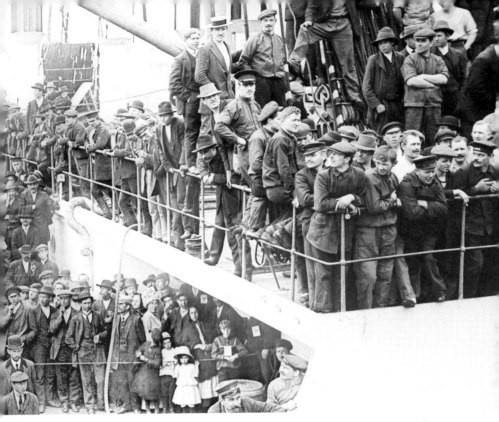

Annie and her brothers traveled in steerage, where the accommodations were dirty, dark, and cramped.

On most boats, people in steerage shared a single space crammed with bunk beds. They had to cook for themselves. People often became ill from being in such close quarters with so many people, or from sea sickness.

However, for many people, the difficult journey was worth it. After a week or so of rough sailing, they would arrive at Ellis Island: the first stop in their new lives.

The world's largest ocean liner at the time, *Imperator*, brought over 4,000 passengers from Europe to New York Harbor on June 19, 1913.

A Shiny Statue
When Annie arrived in the US, the Statue of Liberty was a shiny orange color! The statue, a gift to the US from France in 1885, is made of copper. When copper spends time in contact with oxygen, it acquires a green rust-like covering. By 1906, the statue had turned the blue-green color you see today.

ELLIS ISLAND AT LAST

After many long days at sea, the ship's bell rang to announce the arrival of Annie's ship! Passengers rushed to the deck, crowding for a first look at their new home. In the distance, an impressive sight caught Annie's eye: the Statue of Liberty.

For Annie and the other immigrants arriving at Ellis Island, disembarking the ship meant more than just the relief of setting foot on land. They would be taking their first steps in their new home country.

A Growing Island
To keep up with growing immigration numbers, the US government had Ellis Island itself expanded. They added dirt to create more land.

Immigrants arriving at Ellis Island around 1905

43

Citizenship
Some new immigrants wanted to become full US citizens. As citizens, they would have the same rights and responsibilities as the other members of the nation. To gain citizenship, immigrants had to apply through the court system.

Immigrants in line to meet with officials at Ellis Island, 1930s

Before Annie and her brothers could start their new lives, they had to be approved by the officials at Ellis Island. Today, immigrants—and even travelers—need many government documents to enter foreign countries. But for decades, these documents weren't required—and some didn't exist! People who were approved at an immigration station could simply go on to live in the US.

Changing Times
With the Immigration Act of 1924, the US government severely limited the number of people allowed to immigrate to the US. This act was reversed in 1965, allowing people to immigrate freely once again. But for various reasons, immigration has remained a debated subject, and over the decades, laws both restricting and supporting immigration have continued to be put into effect.

In the US, the first passports, or documents that show someone is a citizen of a country, appeared in 1789. But it wasn't until the middle of the 20th century that they became necessary to enter or leave the country. And until 1924, most immigrants to the US did not need any documents at all. After that, though, people entering the country were required to have a visa, an official document stating that the person is allowed to enter.

45

Quarantine History

The idea of quarantining people to keep others from getting sick is centuries old. To stop a plague from spreading in Venice, Italy, around the year 1348, ships had to wait 40 days before entering the harbor. The word *quarantine* comes from the Italian word *quarantena*, which means "a period of 40 days."

Annie and her brothers had to wait in line to receive health checks. Each person arriving at Ellis Island was required to pass a medical examination to make sure they had no illnesses or diseases. Sick people were sent to a hospital on the island for treatment. Sometimes, they were placed in quarantine, but once they had recovered, most were allowed to continue on into the country.

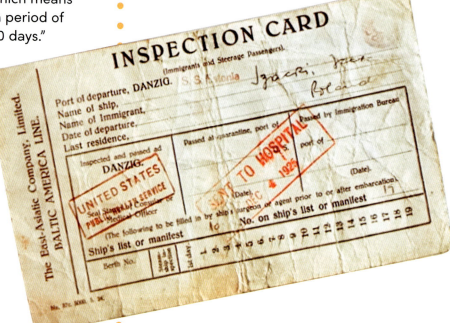

Children receiving health checks, 1911

Government workers were also on the lookout for people with physical or mental disabilities. People who were not considered "fit" to work were often unfairly detained or sent back to their countries of origin. Today, we call such discrimination "ableism."

Special Treatment
Passengers who had booked first- or second-class tickets were dropped off at different piers in New York, where they only had to pass through a very quick inspection point.

Changing Names
You might have heard that American workers at Ellis Island often changed immigrants' names to seem "more American," or that names were mistranslated because many immigrants weren't able to read or write. But those are myths! Records show that people immigrating through Ellis Island kept the names they arrived with. Later, some chose to change their own names, possibly to "fit in" to American culture.

After passing their health check, Annie and her brothers had to answer some questions. The interview confirmed their identities and made sure all their travel information was correct. Such interviews also identified people who might be considered dangerous.

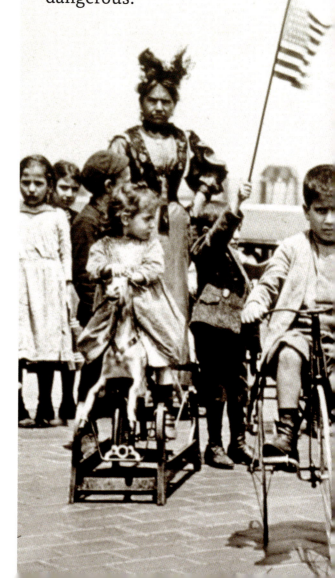

What might make a person dangerous? The government wanted to keep out people who had broken laws in their countries. Of course, very few immigrants were criminals. Even so, the interviews must have made Annie and her brothers nervous!

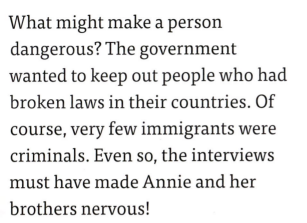

Families wait on a rooftop garden at Ellis Island around 1900.

Curious Questions

Most interviews involved 29 questions, including:

1. Where were you born?
2. Are you married?
3. What is your job?
4. Have you ever been convicted of a crime?
5. How much money do you have?
6. What is your destination?

Stuck on Angel Island
At Angel Island in California, immigrants were regularly detained for weeks, months, or in a few cases years, in uncomfortable quarters. Racism and prejudice against Asian people—and in the late 19th and early 20th centuries, Chinese people in particular—were widespread in the US.

If a person was suspected to be dangerous, was considered unfit to work, or had an illness that worried US officials, that person might have been held at Ellis Island. Some people were sent back to their home countries. But almost all who arrived at Ellis Island passed through the station within a few hours.

Newcomers await questioning in the Registry Room at Ellis Island, 1912.

After several long hours, the decision was made: Annie and her brothers had passed! On January 1, 1892, Annie Moore became the first person to immigrate through Ellis Island. Her brothers followed her shortly. It was time to begin their lives in the US!

A Happy Reunion
Many immigrants, including Annie's family, met up with friends or family who came to Ellis Island to meet them. One spot where families met had so many happy reunions that it became known as the "kissing post."

A Little Italy
Many Italian immigrants who journeyed through Ellis Island chose to stay in New York City. Some opened their own restaurants or grocery stores. So many Italian people moved into one area that the neighborhood became known as Little Italy.

A NEW LIFE

For Annie and her family, the long journey to Ellis Island came to a happy end. They had made the decision to leave their home country. They had packed up what belongings they could. And they had spent days or weeks traveling. Now, they had arrived! But what was next?

Many immigrants—including Annie and her family—stayed in New York City. Others moved to states that had jobs available. Jobs were not always easy to find, though, especially if the immigrants did not know how to speak English. Many immigrants worked hard labor jobs, like mining, construction, or building railroads. Others used the specialized skills they brought from home and became clothing makers, bakers, woodworkers, and more.

The Annie Moore Monument in Cobh, Ireland

Mulberry Street, New York City, around 1900

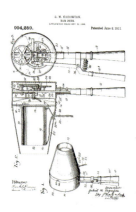

Immigrant Inventors
According to one study, new immigrants made up nearly 20 percent of American inventors between 1880 and 1940! Immigrants created amazing innovations we now take for granted—like the handheld hair dryer, invented by Armenian immigrant Gabriel Kazanjian.

Things were not always easy for immigrants in their new lives. In fact, life in the US could be very difficult. Immigrants often did not speak the local language. Local laws, rules, customs, behaviors, and traditions were unfamiliar to them and could be confusing.

Jewish market and tenement houses, New York City, around 1905

Tenement Housing
In New York City, many immigrants lived in tenement houses. These were cramped, narrow apartment buildings, often kept in bad or unsafe condition.

Americans were not always friendly to new immigrants. Many Americans held stereotypes, overly simple or untrue beliefs, about people from different countries. Some Americans worried that immigrants would take jobs away from them. Because immigrants usually did not have very much money, they often had to live in poor or unsafe areas—sometimes because Americans did not allow them to live elsewhere.

A young Russian woman at Ellis Island, 1905

Sentiment Today
Anti-immigrant sentiment remains a part of modern American life. While many leaders, politicians, and communities call for welcoming immigrants into the country, others seek to restrict immigration.

Immigrants to the US often faced anti-immigrant sentiment, or the attitudes and beliefs of local people that immigrants should not be welcome. In the 1920s, anti-immigrant sentiment became so strong that the US government passed laws to try to keep immigrants out. Some shop owners and businesses banned immigrants from entering. Many immigrants faced physical attacks.

Unfair Laws
In 1882, the government passed the Chinese Exclusion Act, which made it difficult for Chinese people to enter the US and nearly impossible for them to become American citizens. The law was not repealed until 1943.

Despite various challenges, immigrants did not give up. They worked hard to make better lives for themselves and their children—and for everyone in the US! Immigrants helped build important things like subways and railroads. They helped pave streets. They worked in mines and on farms.

Creating Kindness
Although many Americans discriminated against new immigrants, others were welcoming. Many people and businesses were grateful for the labor immigrants took on. Some invited immigrant families to join local activities and organizations. Some churches and other places of worship welcomed new immigrants by providing clothing and food.

Italian immigrants building a railroad in New York around 1900

Famous Foods
One of the most iconic US foods was introduced by immigrants! In the 1860s, German immigrants began selling small sausage sandwiches— now known as hot dogs. Another popular food—the fortune cookie— was created in 1914 by a Japanese chef living in San Francisco.

As immigrants from different countries settled across the US, they adapted to an American way of life. But they weren't always happy about it. Many immigrants felt forced to change themselves to fit in and be successful. They didn't feel welcome to practice their own traditions, speak their own languages, or wear their home country's fashions.

A woman arriving at Ellis Island around 1925

This 2016 New York City mural by the French street artist JR features immigrant children from Ellis Island.

At the same time, many immigrants did maintain and share their own cultures and traditions. People across the country began to eat new foods, like pizza. They started listening to new types of music, like polka from Eastern Europe. And people blended parts of their different cultures together to create new things! This blending of cultural elements is known as cultural fusion. Modern American culture has been created by the blending of many different cultures and peoples.

Lots of Lox
Today, many people enjoy a meal known as bagels and lox (smoked salmon). Bagels came to the US with Jewish immigrants. But did you know that lox came with Scandinavian immigrants? As the two cultures mingled in the US, the foods began to be eaten together.

The End of Ellis Island
After the US government passed the Immigration Act of 1924, immigration to the US trickled to a halt.

Luggage left by immigrants who came through Ellis Island, on display at the museum

Ellis Island is no longer active as an immigration station. In 1965, the site became a National Park, and in 1976, it opened to the public as a museum. The site remains an important part of American history. That's because its effects can still be seen today.

From building the roads that pave the nation to shaping the

many different cultures present in the US, the immigrants who passed through Ellis Island had a powerful effect. Today, Ellis Island reminds us that people can choose to come together to create new futures for themselves and that immigrants have shaped—and continue to shape—the country in many ways.

New US citizens are sworn in during a special ceremony at Ellis Island in 2016.

GLOSSARY

Ableism
Discrimination against people with physical or mental disabilities

Antisemitism
Prejudice against or hatred of Jewish people

Colonize
To forcibly take control of an area and its people

Country of origin
The birthplace of a person who has moved to another country

Detain
To keep or hold

Economy
The state of a country's wealth, resources, and business

Emigrate
To move away from one's home country

Famine
A lack of food throughout an area

Federal
Related to the government of a country

Genocide
The deliberate destruction of a certain group of people

Immigrate
To move to another country to live permanently

Persecution
Harassment of, or violence toward, those who have a different background, identity, religion, or political views

Plague
A contagious disease that spreads quickly among many people

Pogrom
An outbreak of organized violence against a certain ethnic group

Port
A town, city, or harbor where ships unload

Quarantine
To keep sick people separated from others to avoid spreading disease

Refugee
A person who leaves their home country to escape a dangerous situation

Religious freedom
The legal ability to practice or not practice any religion

Steamship
A boat or ship that is powered by a steam engine

Steerage
The part of the ship reserved for people with the least-expensive tickets

Tsunami
A massive ocean wave usually caused by an earthquake or volcanic eruption

INDEX

ableism 47
Angel Island Immigration Station 11, 23, 25, 32, 50
antisemitism 20
Armenian immigrants 26, 54
bagels 21
Bell, Alexander Graham 15
Castle Garden, New York City 28, 31
Chadekel family 20
Chinese immigrants
  immigrant spotlights 25, 32
  jobs 27, 33
  port of entry 11
  racism against 50, 56
  reasons for emigrating 16
citizenship 44, 56, 61
cultural fusion 59
Dowleyne, Ella 34
economy 24–25
Ellis Island Immigration Station
  busiest day 13
  fire 30
  health checks 46–47
  immigrants arriving at 9, 13, 36, 42–44
  immigrants turned away 12, 50
  interpreters 8
  interviews 48–49
  modern building 6, 12
  museum 60
  name 29
  number of immigrants received 13, 29
  official opening 30
  original building 7
emigration 23

enslaved people 10, 24, 35
foods, brought by immigrants 18, 21, 58–59
fortune cookies 58
genocide 26
German immigrants 33, 58
Gold Rush 24
Hong, Edward 32
hot dogs 58
immigrants
  arriving at Ellis Island 9, 13, 36, 42–44
  changing names 48
  colonizing Indigenous nations 7
  definition of 7
  difficulties for 54–58
  inventors 15, 54
  jobs 52, 57
  journey to Ellis Island 8, 32–41
  laws about 45, 56, 60
  leaving home 14–23
  official entry points 10, 11
  turned away from Ellis Island 12, 50
Imperator 41
Indigenous peoples 7, 9, 24
interpreters 8
inventions 15, 33, 54
Irish immigrants 16–17, 33 *see also* Moore, Annie
Italian immigrants 18–19, 52, 57
Japanese immigrants 11, 58
Jewish immigrants 20–22, 55, 59
journey to Ellis Island 8, 32–41

Jue family 25
Kazanjian, Gabriel 54
Kelly-Grimm, Tilda de Mello 19
language interpreters 8
Lenape people 7
lox 59
Macdonald, Daniel 17
Mexican immigrants 11, 23
Moore, Annie
  arrival at Ellis Island 42, 44, 46, 48–49
  family in US 27, 34, 51
  immigration through Ellis Island 7, 51
  journey to Ellis Island 8, 11, 34–36, 41
  new life in US 52
  statue 52
Native Americans 7, 9, 24
New Orleans, Louisiana 35
New York City 21, 52, 55
Ottoman Empire 26
persecution 26
pizza 18
pogroms 20
potato blight 16–17
quarantine 46
railroads 15, 33, 57
refugees 22–23
religious freedom 27
Statue of Liberty 8, 42
steamships 33–34, 38–41
steerage 40–41
telephones 15
tenement houses 55
Thomas family 14
Titanic 38–39
toys 36
Transcontinental Railroad 15, 33

63

QUIZ

Answer the questions to see what you have learned. Check your answers in the key below.

1. What year did Ellis Island open?

2. Who was the first person to immigrate to the US through Ellis Island?

3. True or False: People have always needed a passport to immigrate to the US.

4. True or False: About 98 percent of immigrants to Ellis Island were allowed to enter the country.

5. What year did Ellis Island become a national park?

1. 1892 2. Annie Moore 3. False 4. True 5. 1965